FERDINAND
MAGELLAN

What Made Them Great

Scott Brewster

Illustrated by Severino Baraldi

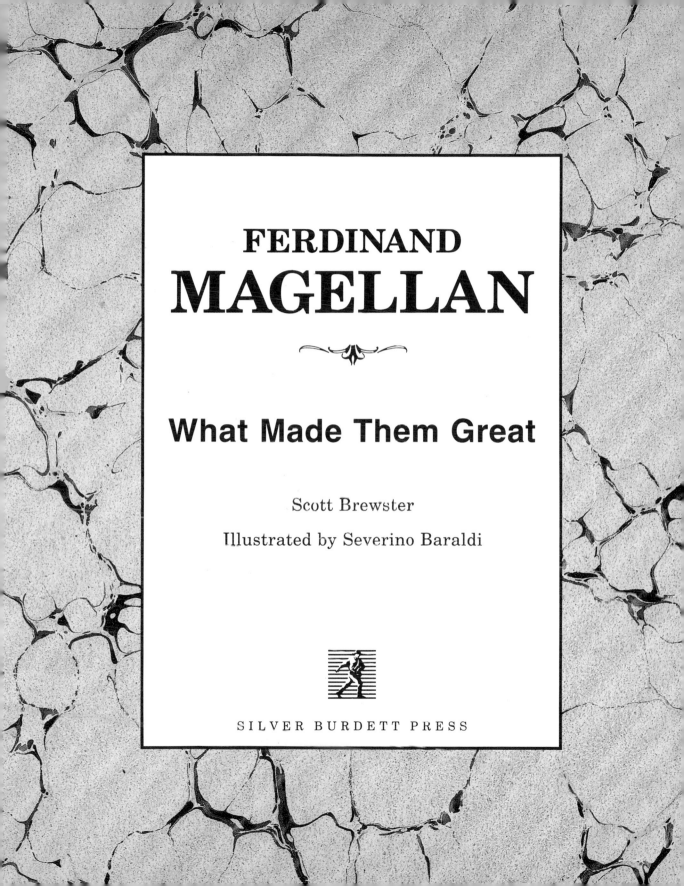

SILVER BURDETT PRESS

FERDINAND
MAGELLAN

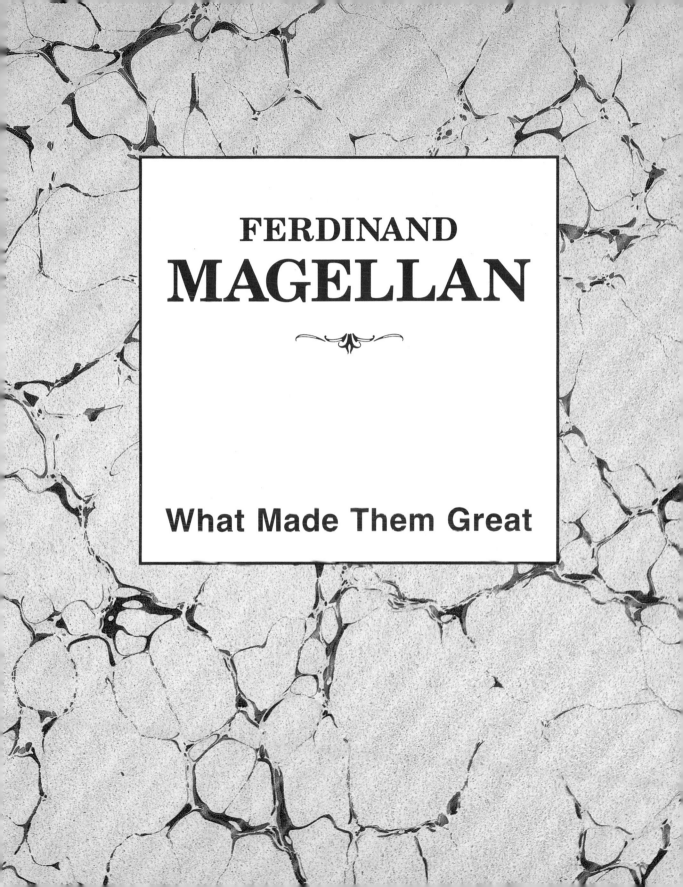

What Made Them Great

ACKNOWLEDGMENTS

We would like to thank Vincent Cassidy, Department of History, University of Akron, and Verna Mair, Library Consultant, Aldine I.S.D., Texas, for their guidance and helpful suggestions.

Project Editor: Emily Easton (Silver Burdett Press)

Adapted and reformatted from the original by
Kirchoff/Wohlberg, Inc.

Project Director: John R. Whitman
Graphics Coordinator: Jessica A. Kirchoff
Production Coordinator: Marianne Hile

Library of Congress Cataloging-in-Publication Data

Brewster, Scott,
    Ferdinand Magellan/Scott Brewster; illustrated by Severino Baraldi.
    p. cm.—[FROM SERIES: What Made Them Great]

Adaptation of: Magellano/Sergio Bitossi; translated by Stephen Thorne.
    © 1985 Silver Burdett Company, Morristown, New Jersey.
    [FROM SERIES: Why They Became Famous]
    Includes bibliographical references.
Summary: Recounts how the sixteenth-century Portuguese explorer launched the first voyage
    around the world, although he met his death before his men completed the expedition.
    1. Magalhães, Fernão de, d. 1521—Juvenile literature. 2. Explorers—Portugal—Biography—
    Juvenile literature. 3. Voyages around the world—Juvenile literature. [1. Magellan, Ferdinand,
    d. 1521. 2. Explorers. 3. Voyages around the world.] I. Baraldi, Severino, ill. II. Bitossi, Sergio.
    Perché Sono Diventati Famosi, Magellano. III. Title. IV. Series.

G286.M2B74 1990   910'.92—dc20   [B]   [92]   89-77114   CIP   AC

© Fabbri Editori S.p.A., Milan 1982
Translated into English by Stephen Thorne for Silver Burdett Press
from Perché Sono Diventati Famosi: Magellano
First published in Italy in 1982 by Fabbri Editori S.p.A., Milan

10 9 8 7 6 5 4 3 2 1 (Library Binding)
10 9 8 7 6 5 4 3 2 1 (Softcover)

ISBN 0-382-09979-6 (Library Binding)
ISBN 0-382-24005-7 (Softcover)

TABLE OF CONTENTS

A Restless Soldier
and Sailor

he voyage began on September 20, 1519.
At the Spanish seaport of San Lucar de
Barrameda, a fleet of five ships was
preparing to set sail. The ships were the *Trinidad,*
the *San Antonio,* the *Concepcion,* the *Santiago,* and
the *Victoria.* About 250 men were on board. Most of
them were Spanish. A few were Portuguese. The rest
came from various other countries. There was even a
gunner from England.

On the dock, the crowd cheered. An ocean
breeze filled the sails. Soon, the ships were rolling
out bravely into the Atlantic Ocean. People
continued to wave. Nobody could guess that the
voyage would end in triumph— and in tragedy. None
of the five captains would return. Only one of the
ships would complete the voyage. She would carry
eighteen sailors. These men would be the only
survivors of the first voyage around the world.

In command of this Spanish expedition was a
Portuguese captain, Ferdinand Magellan. He was an
experienced sailor and a tough commander. Some
people admired him because he was daring and
intelligent. Magellan had a dramatic plan. He
intended to reach the Spice Islands, in the Orient, by

sailing west across the Atlantic. When he reached the New World, he would hunt for a passage leading to the Pacific Ocean.

Of course, nobody knew if such a passage even existed. But Magellan believed that there must be a passage. What's more, he felt certain that he could find it.

At this time in history, world exploration was a great challenge. Spain and Portugal led the way. Portuguese sea captains had already reached the Moluccas, known as the Spice Islands. However, they had sailed east, not west. Thirty years earlier, Bartholomew Dias had sailed around the southern tip of Africa, and from there into the Indian Ocean. The following year—in 1498—Vasco da Gama navigated the Indian Ocean and continued to India. In 1509, Lopez de Sequeira rounded India and crossed the Bay of Bengal, reaching Malacca on the Malay Peninsula.

Meanwhile, Christopher Columbus had sailed boldly across the Atlantic in 1492. The lands he discovered in the New World now belonged to Spain.

Not surprisingly, Spain and Portugal had become bitter rivals. There was no open warfare, but they were enemies. In the Treaty of Tordesillas, they agreed to divide their discoveries. A line was drawn around the world from north to south. It cut through the "hump" of South America. Everything east of the line went to Portugal. Lands lying west of the line would belong to Spain.

The Tordesillas line solved the problem in the New World. But how did it affect the Spice Islands, which were on the other side of the world? Nobody was exactly sure. Geographers and scientists did not know how wide the Pacific Ocean was.

Magellan believed that the Spice Islands were on the Spanish side of the Tordesillas line. This was one reason why the king of Spain was so willing to pay for Magellan's costly expedition.

From the outset of the voyage, trouble began brewing. Magellan was Portuguese. All of his captains were Spanish. Not surprisingly, they did not trust Magellan. It was whispered that he was really loyal to Portugal.

Before the departure from San Lucar, Magellan had called his captains together. He announced that he planned to attempt something never done before. "We are going to sail around the world," he said. "We'll sail west across the Atlantic and keep going until we get home again."

It was a dangerous and daring plan. Many among the captains and crew on the five vessels thought the idea was insane. However, none of the Spanish captains decided to back out. They were willing to follow Magellan and to see how he handled the fleet. At the same time, they planned to watch him with special care. Boldly, the ships put out to sea.

Who was Ferdinand Magellan? And how did a Portuguese captain win command of a Spanish fleet? He was born about 1480 in Oporto. His family belonged to the lower nobility. As a child, he became a page in the royal household of the queen of Portugal.

After he grew up, he left the court and went to sea, often on warships. At the age of twenty-five, he joined an expedition going to India. On the way, he

took part in the capture of Mombasa on the coast of East Africa. He was wounded in a battle off the Malabar Coast. He also saw action in a naval battle near Diu, off the coast of India. There the Portuguese defeated Egyptian and Indian fleets.

In 1511, the Portuguese captured Malacca on the Malay Peninsula that extends south between Sumatra and Borneo. This victory paved the way for a chance to conquer the famous Spice Islands, which are located in modern-day Indonesia. The battle for Malacca turned out to be a turning point in Magellan's life. As a reward for fighting so bravely, he was made an officer.

Meanwhile, Magellan's reputation kept growing. By the age of thirty-one, he was looking ahead. To become an explorer was his ambition. His knowledge of sailing ships increased each year. He had visited many foreign lands. He knew all the harbors along the shores of Africa, India, and the

Malay Peninsula. Luckily,
much of the earth's
surface remained to be
explored. What he lacked,
however, was a ship of his own.
     In Malacca, Magellan
had a chance to meet some
of the people living on the
Malay Peninsula. Now and
then, their leaders came on
board the Portuguese ships.
The Malays were eager to
trade spices and gold for
Western goods. And

Europeans were eager to obtain spices. This was because spices were used as food preservatives, as well as to help add flavor.

But Magellan's days in Malacca were cut short. Some of the sailors were jealous of his success with the Malays. They convinced his commander to send him back to Lisbon in disgrace. But Portugal's King Manuel needed Magellan's battle skills. Portugal held land in North Africa, as well as in the Far East. When fighting broke out with the Moors, Magellan was sent to Morocco. His leg was wounded in the Battle of Azimur. This time, his wound was serious. For the rest of his life, he walked with a limp.

Magellan's misfortune continued. In Morocco, he was guarding sheep and cattle captured from the enemy. Some of the livestock vanished. He was accused of selling the animals back to the Moors and pocketing the money. Indignant, Magellan hurried home to defend himself. He asked King Manuel to have the charges withdrawn. But the king sent him back to Morocco. The matter would be investigated.

In the end, Magellan was cleared of any wrongdoing. He returned to Lisbon, and sought a command at sea, where he felt more at home.

Lisbon was full of news about explorations. Expeditions were departing for unknown regions of the earth. And other ships headed for distant lands already discovered by Portugal. It was not hard to meet sailors with exciting tales of their adventures. Magellan could not help envying them.

Magellan had served his king and country faithfully. On his body, he bore the scars of wounds suffered in battle. Few sailors knew the Far East as well as he did. Very likely, he must have felt that he deserved to command a sailing ship.

However, little is known about Magellan's thinking. He was a person who didn't like to talk about himself. Many would come to admire him. But few were able to get close to him. Even his best friends knew little about his early life, only what they had seen for themselves. One man who knew him fairly well was Antonio Pigafetta, a writer who traveled with Magellan on his great voyage. In Pigafetta's glowing words, Magellan is called "so noble a Captain." But the chronicler gives no details about Magellan's life before the voyage began.

"Magellan," said one of his acquaintances, "is a man of few words. He keeps to himself and seems to think of nothing but going to sea again. Those who have seen him in action consider him a great leader. He is afraid of nothing."

One of his friends was named Francisco Serrão. They had fought together at the battle of Malacca in Malay. Magellan saved Serrão's life. Later, Serrão wrote to Magellan, "I remember that when I fell, you beat back the Malayans with your

sword. I hope the day will come when you will sail to the Spice Islands."

It was amazing how much progress was being made in world exploration. With each passing decade, the map of the earth was being filled in. Still, a huge amount of land was still uncharted.

More than anything, Magellan wanted a promotion to sea captain. But it was not his only motive. More important was exploration. He was a true child of the Age of Discovery. He longed to capture the attention of the world with sensational feats. There were plenty of heroes to use as models. Da Gama had sailed to India. Columbus had discovered the Americas. Why shouldn't Ferdinand Magellan take his place alongside of such renowned men?

At that time, the Americas intrigued many people. But not Magellan. His thoughts constantly turned to the East Indies. This was an enormous area, not yet visited by many Europeans. Magellan felt lucky to have already traveled there. That was why he believed his best chances for success lay in that direction.

Besides, the Spice Islands were fabulously rich. This might help to gain a sponsor for a more ambitious voyage. Just one shipload of spices from the Moluccas would pay for the cost of an expedition many times over.

"The World Is Round, and I'll Prove It!"

No explorer could lead an expedition without permission from the king. The ruler of Portugal was King Manuel I. The discovery of new lands to add to his empire interested Manuel a great deal. It was he who had approved the voyages of Vasco da Gama and also of Alfonso de Albuquerque, who had captured Malacca. Magellan requested a meeting with the king.

In 1516, King Manuel received him at the royal court in Lisbon. Manuel was clad in splendid robes. A crown sat on his head. Around the throne gathered his advisers. As custom required, Magellan knelt.

Then, it came time to explain his idea. He wanted to lead an expedition around Africa and India to the Spice Islands, Magellan said. His plan would surely increase Portuguese trade. He also promised to look for unknown lands east of the Moluccas. Of course, his voyage would add immensely to the glory of Portugal and to her king.

Manuel listened carefully. Magellan was not a stranger to him. The king remembered that Magellan had once been a page for his mother, the queen of Portugal. He also knew perfectly well that

Magellan had fought for him on land and sea. Manuel turned to his chief adviser, who stood next to the throne.

Immediately, the adviser offered an opinion. "Your Majesty, Magellan was accused of selling livestock captured by your troops in Morocco." Magellan could hardly believe his ears. "Your Majesty," he broke in, "I was cleared of that accusation."

"That is true," the king replied.

Frowning, the chief adviser went on. He reminded Manuel that Magellan had gotten into trouble in Malaya. After the battle of Malacca, he had been sent home in disgrace. The king glanced at Magellan, waiting for an explanation.

"Your Majesty, my enemies spread false tales about me," Magellan said. "That was why Albuquerque ordered me home to Lisbon."

"Can you prove that?" snapped the king's adviser.

Magellan hesitated. He finally answered, "No, it's just my word against theirs." This was the simple truth.

Irritated, the king began to shake his head. He had absolute faith in his commanders. In this situation, whose word should he trust? The commanders or the men who served under them? So Manuel decided that the reports about Magellan must be true.

But that was not all. Manuel disliked Magellan. Unlike the king's courtiers, he did not bow and scrape. He spoke his thoughts plainly. And he refused to flatter the king in order to win favor.

Manuel made up his mind to dismiss the sailor. He had other sea captains who could sail to the Indies. He liked any one of them much better than he liked Magellan. "Your appeal is denied," he announced. "You will not command a Portuguese fleet."

Magellan stared at Manuel. Then he answered slowly. "Will your Majesty allow me to offer my services to some other country?" he asked. "They do not seem to be acceptable in my own."

"Do as you please," the king replied angrily. "It does not matter to me where you go."

Insulted, Magellan strode from the palace. He felt he had been treated badly. He also was disappointed about his plan being rejected. Gradually, he shrugged off his feelings of defeat. More determined than ever, he vowed to leave Portugal and look elsewhere for a ship to command.

In the sixteenth century, it was common practice for sea captains to work for countries other than their own. The best example was Columbus, a native of Genoa, Italy. First he tried to get backing from Portugal. After being refused, he went to Spain, where he won the support of Queen Isabella. Magellan, too, decided to try his luck in Spain.

For the time being, however, Magellan stayed in Portugal. He had loaned money to a Lisbon merchant and wanted to collect the debt. During these months, a dramatic new thought occurred to him.

The idea was simple. Instead of traveling east around Africa to the Indies, why not sail in the opposite direction? Magellan could head west across the Atlantic to the New World. From there, he would keep right on going until he reached the Indies. Then, he would continue on around the world.

The more Magellan thought about it, the more confident he grew. Around this time, he received a letter from Francisco Serrão. His friend had decided to live permanently in the Spice Islands. He wrote Magellan that the islands were practically next door to America, only a short voyage across the Pacific.

Of course, Serrão was wrong. But Magellan had no reason not to believe him. Like everyone else, he had a fuzzy idea about the size of the Pacific.

One enormous question remained. How could a ship possibly get from the Atlantic to the Pacific? It couldn't, according to some people. A continent stood in the way. Indeed, many geographers insisted that South America extended all the way down to the Antarctic continent.

Today, we know that it is possible to sail around the capes of both South America and Africa.

But Magellan did not know this. Nor did others to whom he revealed his plan.

One of Magellan's friends was Ruy Faleiro, a mathematician, astronomer, and geographer. Naturally, Faleiro was quick to bring up the problem of South America. "Magellan," he said, "what if South America extends to the South Pole?"

Magellan shrugged. "Even if it does, there must be an opening that connects the Atlantic and the Pacific. I'll have to search along the coast of South America until I find a strait." Ultimately, Magellan was able to convince Faleiro that his plan was sound.

Ruy Faleiro was an odd man. He talked too much. He was quarrelsome. Sometimes, he suffered from attacks of nerves and was unable to work. But he was an expert on maps, especially on new discoveries that were changing the map of the world. He brought Magellan the latest charts and books being published all over Europe.

They argued about the best way to gather money, ships, and men for an expedition. They pored over Faleiro's maps. On the waterfront, they chatted with ship captains just back from the high seas.

Meanwhile, Magellan continued to receive exciting information from his old friend Serrão. A rebel, Serrão had refused to take orders from the Portuguese commander in Malacca. Now, he lived happily on the island of Ternate. In letters to

Magellan, Serrão described his new home as a wonderful paradise.

"The people are charming, the climate is balmy," Serrão wrote. "I am leading the pleasantest life imaginable. Why don't you join me?"

Magellan had no intention of copying Serrão and retiring to the Spice Islands. However, he did want to see the marvels that Serrão described.

In 1517, Magellan and Faleiro traveled to Spain. The year in Lisbon had not been wasted. It had given Magellan time to perfect his plan. By now, he had a good idea of how many ships and men would be needed. He planned to take plenty of European goods that could be traded for spices. So he knew that the holds of the ships would have to be quite spacious.

In Seville, the two men requested an invitation to the Spanish court. Then, they settled down to wait. At that time, Seville was the center where transatlantic voyages were planned. Soon, Magellan and his partner met Juan de Aranda, who was a member of the naval planning board. After hearing Magellan's idea, Aranda was so impressed that he asked to join as a third partner. Getting Aranda's help was a lucky break. His influence at the court was enormous.

A year passed. Magellan and Faleiro decided to switch their loyalty from Portugal to Spain. They promised to become faithful servants of the king.

In Seville, Magellan met Beatriz Barbosa. Her father, an important official, was commander of the royal arsenal. Magellan and Beatriz were married.

Finally, the day came when Magellan and his partners were called to the royal court at Valladolid. They were to meet King Charles I, who would later be crowned Holy Roman Emperor, Charles V. But in 1518, that was two years away.

King Charles listened courteously as Magellan spoke. "Your Majesty," he said, "the Portuguese control the eastern route to the Indies. But the western route lies open to Spain. I will sail it in your name."

Charles asked him, "And if you find the strait through South America? Then what will you do?"

"Circumnavigate the globe," Magellan replied. "I'll sail home by way of the east—from the Spice Islands past India and Africa. The world is round, and I'll prove it!"

King Charles did not need to hear more. "Return to Seville," he told Magellan and his partners. "It is my wish for the planning board to organize the expedition."

Hurrying back to Seville, the three men were very happy. They started making preparations at once. Recruiting men was easy. Word of the new expedition spread rapidly. From all over Europe and North Africa came sailors who wanted to join. Some of them understood Arabic and African languages.

Before long, a crew of more
than 250 was assembled.

It was decided that
Magellan would need five ships.
Unfortunately, the ships
assigned to him were old wrecks.
They had to be fixed up and
made seaworthy. Damaged
planks were replaced in the
hulls. Rigging and sails were
repaired. Decks were scrubbed.
A cannon was installed.

As the work progressed,
Magellan took charge of every
detail. His ships would have to
withstand the pounding of ocean
waves. They would have to ride
out terrible storms. From his
experience aboard many vessels,
Magellan knew exactly what
repairs were needed.

The largest of the five ships
was the *San Antonio*. It weighed
120 tons. Juan de Cartagena
was appointed to be its captain.
Magellan was captain of the
second largest, the *Trinidad*, at

110 tons. The *Concepcion,* 90 tons, was under Gaspar de Quesada. Commanding the smallest ships, the *Victoria* and the *Santiago,* were Luis de Mendoza and Juan Rodriquez Serrano.

Magellan did his best to speed up the departure. Even so, problems kept arising. He ordered supplies to last two years at sea. It was frustrating when provisions failed to arrive on time; or when work was poor and had to be done over.

But the biggest headaches resulted from envy and pride. The Spanish kept increasing the power given to Juan de Cartagena, captain of the *San Antonio.* Before long, Cartagena's power was beginning to rival Magellan's. Or so it seemed.

Other captains complained that there were too many Portuguese sailors among the crews. They insisted on recruiting more Spaniards, Italians, Germans, and Flemish.

In one respect, their demands had a happy outcome. Among the Italians was Antonio Pigafetta, who was to act as Magellan's secretary. Another person might have supplied ordinary information. But thanks to Pigafetta, there remains a stunning account of Magellan's adventures.

The waiting ended. Raising anchor at Seville, the fleet moved down the Guadalquiver River to San Lucar de Barrameda. On September 20, 1519, it swept out into the Atlantic.

Mutinies and a Search for the Strait

fter leaving San Lucar, the fleet turned southwest toward the Canary Islands. The Canaries were located in the Atlantic, off the coast of Africa. In 1479, there had been an agreement between Spain and Portugal. Ever since, the islands had belonged to the Spanish. Owning the islands had turned out to be fortunate. Like other Spanish captains setting out on long voyages, Magellan made his first stop at the Canaries.

Dropping anchor in the harbor of Tenerife, he ordered his ships to restock with fresh water and meat. During the layover, the crews witnessed a strange sight. Afterward, it would be called a "miracle." Towards midday, a thick cloud descended on one of the islands. The cloud almost touched the ground. It settled on a huge tree whose leaves started to drip water. More incredible, the water ran down the tree trunk to the ground. Local people rushed up to collect water at the foot of the tree.

The "raintree" interested Antonio Pigafetta. In his journal, he wrote that the stream of water flowed profusely. Human beings and animals drank as much as they wanted. But Pigafetta did not believe that the weeping tree was a miracle. He treated it as some natural phenomenon.

Soon the Canaries were left behind. As the fleet rolled southwest between the Cape Verde Islands and the coast of Africa, another odd event took place. The crews quickly forgot about the raintree.

One night after a heavy storm, the *Trinidad* was suddenly bathed in a fiery glow. This phenomenon, known to sailors as St. Elmo's fire, is well known to modern science. It is caused by electrical conditions in the atmosphere. But in the sixteenth century, it was considered a marvel. For two hours, St. Elmo's fire enveloped the main mast of Magellan's flagship. Even Pigafetta grew alarmed. At last, the sea grew calm and the fire vanished. Everybody felt relieved.

However, Magellan had other worries on his mind. Already, his leadership was being challenged by Juan de Cartagena, captain of the *San Antonio.* Cartagena believed that Magellan was sticking too close to the coast of Africa. In his opinion, Magellan would be better off heading directly for South America. Cartagena decided to voice his doubts.

Bringing the *San Antonio* close to the *Trinidad,* he called out that the captain-general was taking the wrong direction. In the course of the conversation, Cartagena was disrespectful. For one thing, he had forgotten that he was supposed to

salute Magellan. One of the rules required that each of the four captains salute Magellan aboard the flagship every evening. Instead, Cartagena began to ridicule Magellan.

. Magellan was furious. Shortly after this incident, all four captains came in small boats to attend a meeting. When they climbed aboard the *Trinidad,* Magellan gave orders for Cartagena's arrest.

Now, Cartagena lost his temper. He argued. Then, he tried to win the support of the others. "Fellow Spaniards," he said to them, "you know I'm right. This Portuguese fool is off course. Stand by me, and I'll take us to South America."

"According to my charts," Magellan said sharply, "we're on the right course." No, he would say nothing more. Details would be revealed later.

In the end, the captains obeyed Magellan. They refused to listen to Cartagena. Standing silently, they watched as he was taken aboard the *Victoria* as a prisoner. The command of the *San Antonio* was switched to another Spanish officer, Antonio de Coca.

The captains returned to their ships. The voyage resumed. Magellan followed his charts, turning the ships toward South America when he had reached the correct point.

Although Magellan had won, he had cause to be nervous. The Spanish captains had given in, but they were extremely unhappy. In the privacy of their own ships, they constantly criticized their commander. There was angry talk of desertion. Rumors got back to Magellan. But he did not care so long as they obeyed him and followed the flagship. At night, lights burned on the stern of the *Trinidad*. The other ships could not pretend they had become lost in the darkness.

The fleet continued across the Atlantic. Frightening storms battered the ships. Even more terrifying were the calms. At these times, the ships were unable to move. There was absolutely no wind to fill their sails and push them forward.

Finally, there came a day when a cry went up from the lookouts in the crow's nests. They had reached the coast of South America and Brazil. Discovered by Pedro Cabral in 1500, this huge territory had been claimed by the Portuguese.

In size, Brazil was far larger than Portugal itself. Even Pigafetta was awed. As he wrote in his journal, "That land of Verzin (Brazil) is wealthier and larger than Spain, France, and Italy put together. It belongs to the king of Portugal."

So far, the Portuguese had done almost nothing about establishing settlements. This was lucky for Magellan. Without risk of danger, he was able to anchor his fleet near the site of Rio de Janeiro. No Portuguese were there to object that he was trespassing. Magellan was happy to order a

break in the voyage. In this land of sun, his crews could relax for a while. When everyone was rested, they would turn south and search for the strait leading to the Pacific.

It was a pleasure to visit Brazil. The native people were unbelievably friendly. Pigafetta described them as handsome and healthy. He believed most Brazilians lived until the ages of 125 to 140. This was an exaggeration, of course.

But many of his other comments were accurate.

For example, the chronicler wrote that they were Stone Age people, who knew nothing about the use of metal. The women cultivated the fields. The men went out in their canoes and fished.

Both sexes liked to decorate themselves with parrot feathers. Pigafetta admired their looks. "Men and women are as well proportioned as we," he decided.

The Brazilians also were generous. They built the Spanish a house, probably assuming they would be staying. When they learned the visitors were leaving, they presented a large gift of brazilwood. This particular wood produced a brilliant red dye. The Brazilians valued the dye greatly. Therefore, the brazilwood was a generous gift that expressed their goodwill.

Brazil was rich in all kinds of foods. When it was time to go, the ships were loaded with fruit and vegetables. These two foods were extremely important on long expeditions like Magellan's. Without fresh fruits and vegetables to eat, sailors eventually fell ill with a disease called scurvy. Unknown to Magellan and people of his century, scurvy is caused by a lack of vitamin C in the diet. This vitamin is found in fruits and vegetables.

To give thanks and to ask for divine help, a special Mass was said. The ships had been overhauled. The holds were full of food. Magellan's ships got under way. By January 10, 1520, the fleet reached the mouth of the River Plate. It was so wide that at first Magellan thought this might be the passage into the Pacific.

Sailing up the river proved a bitter disappointment. As Magellan went on, he had to face the truth. It was only a river. Besides, the water was fresh. In a real strait, the water would taste salty from the sea.

As he moved along the coast of South America, Magellan had to sail blind. There were no charts or maps to guide him. And in fact, no explorer had ever reported a strait. So Magellan was obliged to explore every opening.

To his crews, Magellan seemed completely sure of himself. Yet, there must have been times when his confidence weakened. Did he wonder if he could be wrong? Had he led all these men astray?

Still, he kept moving onward. Magellan was a man with a vision. And he was extremely stubborn. Like Columbus, he refused to believe that his ideas could be wrong. Both men were driven to follow their visions to the end.

Magellan's problem was different from Columbus's. There was no question that Magellan had reached South America. He would not stumble across any new land masses. But he did dream of finding a strait. Magellan could not prove that the strait really existed. But in his mind's eye, he could see it.

That winter, he pushed the bow of the *Trinidad* into one passage after another. Each

proved to be a dead end. By night, he sat alone in his cabin. He mulled over the problem and said his prayers faithfully. When everything human seemed to fail him, he asked for divine help.

Once again, the crews began to grow restless and suspicious. On the other ships, the Spanish captains whispered behind Magellan's back. The voyage was lagging behind schedule. By now they should be in the Pacific. For that matter, was there any strait? Or did it exist only in the captain-general's imagination? As the weeks passed, those questions were asked more and more frequently.

The stories grew wilder. Some of the men insisted that Magellan was plotting against them. It was said that he secretly planned to abandon the other four vessels. Then, he would take his flagship back to Portugal.

Magellan realized that his men had begun to doubt him. When he appeared on deck to check his lists of supplies, he could sense their fears. Whenever he got the chance, he offered encouragement. "We've come this far together," he would say. "Let us go on together." But his words had little effect.

As the ships traveled south, heavy gales ripped at the sails. Freezing winds swept the decks. Stinging sleet and snowflakes chilled the men to the bone. They had never expected to travel this far south. Their clothing was too thin for the brutal cold.

The solid gray sky lowered over the fleet like a funeral shroud. Now and then, gigantic icebergs floated by. The helmsmen struggled to avoid hitting them.

In the Antarctic, they passed islands inhabited by vast numbers of penguins. Fresh meat was in short supply. The sailors caught penguins by the dozens. They skinned the birds even before removing the feathers. Hunger was fierce. But the cold was

even worse. Magellan's men were suffering cruelly. He began looking for an inlet where they could stop and seek shelter. Eventually, the weather would have to turn warmer.

On March 31, 1520, he ordered his captains to drop anchor. The spot where they stopped is the Bay of San Julian, on the coast of what is now Argentina.

On shore appeared an unbelievably tall man. He was a giant. His face was painted red. Yellow circles ringed his eyes. Two hearts were painted in the middle of his cheeks. His hair was dyed white, and he wore practically no clothing. Despite the cold, his only garment was a moth-eaten skin.

A party of sailors hastened ashore. When the giant saw them, he began to dance and sing. He threw sand and dust over his head. He seemed to be suffering some kind of fit. The sailors showed the dancing man a mirror. His reaction was comical. Upon seeing his reflection, he leaped backwards and nearly fell flat on the sand. The sailors burst out laughing.

It was the first time the men had laughed in months. Magellan thought this was a good sign. He said to his captains, "We'll winter here."

Fires were built along the shore. More natives appeared. They were curious to meet the men from the sea. For a little while, everything went smoothly. One giant agreed to become a Christian and was baptized John. But then, fighting broke out. A Spaniard was shot by an arrow and died. The sailors killed some of the natives and imprisoned others.

The next day, the fight was forgotten. More serious problems had flared up.

Even before leaving Spain, secret resentments had begun to build against Magellan. The trouble came to a head in San Julian Bay. Old conflicts finally burst into the open. The Spanish captains could not understand why the fleet had come so far south without finding a strait. Forming a conspiracy, they decided to mutiny against their commander.

With all his other woes, Magellan found himself in a desperate situation. He faced the danger of losing his fleet and perhaps even his life.

The mutiny began on April 1. It started when a band of men from the *Concepcion* rowed over to the *San Antonio* in a small boat. Their leader was Juan de Cartagena, the rebel captain who had been arrested and imprisoned earlier.

However, Cartagena had managed to escape somehow. This was the second time that he chose to defy Magellan. It seems clear that this time he hoped to be successful in overthrowing the commander. His intention must have been to take over the fleet himself.

At the outset, the mutineers were successful. They easily captured the *San Antonio*. Before long,

the revolt began to spread. Aboard the *Victoria*, some of the crew sided with the conspirators. The captain—Luis de Mendoza—was murdered.

The crews aboard the two rebel ships broke into cheers. "Death to Magellan!" some of the sailors began to shout. "Long live Cartagena!"

Those cheers must have sounded encouraging to Cartagena. For the moment at least, it looked as if he had the upper hand. Three ships—the *Concepcion,* the *San Antonio,* and the *Victoria*—joined his side.

Two ships—the *Trinidad* and the *Santiago*—remained loyal to Magellan.

Magellan was swift to take action. He ordered the mutineers to surrender. Several boats full of armed men were sent across the water. As they approached the rebel ships, it appeared as if they meant to shoot. As a result, the mutineers began to lose their nerve. For all their loud boasting, there were some who had second thoughts.

Magellan's supporters were able to seize the *Victoria*. Now Magellan had three ships against Cartagena's two. With this added strength, Magellan threatened to bombard the rebels with the cannon. Overpowered, the *San Antonio* and the *Concepcion* agreed to surrender.

Soon, it was all over. The mutineers found themselves in chains. Magellan's authority was restored.

One problem still remained. How should the mutineers be punished? In the end, Magellan allowed most of the men to go free. "You were misled by your ringleaders," he told them. "Return to your duties aboard ship, and you will have nothing to fear."

However, the leaders were not treated so kindly. The captain of the *Concepcion* was tried and found guilty of murder. Sentenced to death, he was beheaded on the deck of the *Trinidad.*

Yet another fate awaited Juan de Cartagena. While he had committed no murders, Magellan held him responsible for the uprising. Cartagena was marooned on a deserted island. With him was a priest who had aided him during the mutiny. Food and wine were left for the two men. The fleet sailed away. Neither man was ever heard of again. Obviously, they soon perished.

The mutiny had been crushed. Now, Magellan could continue his hunt for the strait.

One day, he saw a likely passage. He ordered the captain of the *Santiago* to investigate. Without warning, a storm blew up and the small ship was overwhelmed. Near Cape Santa Cruz, the *Santiago* smashed to pieces. Luckily, the crew was able to jump to safety.

Now, only four ships were left. But Magellan never considered turning back. In fact, his confidence had never been higher.

"They won't rebel again," Magellan told one of his officers. "They trust me now. I want to show that their trust is justified."

"The Strait! The Strait!"

On August 24, 1520, the fleet headed for the open sea and swung south. Magellan hoped he would find the passage quickly. All he wanted was to sail through from the Atlantic to the Pacific. Like everyone else in the fleet, he longed to head north to a warmer climate. But if he failed to locate the strait quickly, he was determined to keep hunting. Sooner or later, he would find it.

Progress was slow. At Rio Santa Cruz, Magellan was forced to stop for two months. Again, the crews shivered from icy cold and high winds. Being so near the South Pole made the men nervous and fearful. All around, there was nothing to see but a bleak, barren landscape.

To break the monotony, groups went ashore and fetched wood and fresh water. Sometimes, they fished over the sides of their ships. Otherwise, there was little to do. They hoped that Magellan knew what he was doing.

And yet again, Magellan gave the order to move south. On the feast day of St. Ursula, the fleet rounded a promontory. In the distance stretched the waters of a broad bay.

An officer of the *Trinidad* gazed around impatiently. "How often have we explored bays like this one!" he exclaimed.

"Well, we must explore here, too!" Magellan replied. "The strait might be just in front of us."

The *San Antonio* and the *Concepcion* were sent ahead to explore. The *Trinidad* and *Victoria* dropped anchor and settled down to wait.

A day went by. Aboard the flagship, the men struggled to keep busy. They played cards or dipped fishing lines into the water. As always, they talked about the expedition. In his cabin, Magellan prepared himself for another disappointment. Night dropped.

A second day began. Tension began to mount. Magellan began to pace the deck. Every now and then, he stopped, shading his eyes with his hand. He peered across the water toward the spot where his two ships had last been seen.

Whenever the commander neared, the crew and officers would stop talking. They waited silently until he had gone on. What could they say? Everyone thought he was half-crazed with the idea of finding a passage. And Magellan could read their thoughts, as well. He knew that they were bitter and disappointed.

Overhead, birds swooped and screeched. Waves lapped against the sides of the ships. Sailors spoke in whispered tones. Occasionally, an order rang out. But mostly, the ships were quiet.

Suddenly, the sound of cannon shots rattled across the bay. Men rushed to the sides of the ships.

They scrambled into the rigging. On the highest
deck, Magellan clutched the railing. Moving toward
him across the water came the *San Antonio* and the
Concepcion. Their big guns continued to thunder.

Aboard the *Concepcion,* the lookout shouted
from the crow's nest. "The strait!" he squealed. "The
strait! We've found it!" A roar of triumph rose from
the *Trinidad* and the *Victoria.*

Soon, the captain of the *Concepcion* was
making his report. "It's not a river," he told
Magellan. "The water is salty as the sea."

This was the moment Magellan had been
waiting for. At once, he ordered all four ships into
the strait. Cautiously, the fleet crept forward. On

one side loomed the shadows of overhanging cliffs. On the other side, the fleet dodged rocks and reefs.

It took Magellan a month to lead his ships through the passage. Navigation was tricky. The strait turned out to be more than 300 miles long. In some places it was 15 miles wide.

One day, Magellan sent a boat ahead to explore. Three days later, it returned. After rounding a cape, the sailors had stared in disbelief. Just ahead, just as Magellan had said, the sea stretched ahead to the horizon. It was the great ocean west of the Americas.

When he heard the news, Magellan broke down and wept. He called the passage the "Strait of Patagonia." But geographers would later name it in honor of the explorer himself—the "Strait of Magellan." The fleet left the strait and entered the western ocean. The surface was so smooth and peaceful that Magellan called it the "Pacific Ocean."

Amid the excitement, the *San Antonio* disappeared. Unknown to Magellan, a band of rebel sailors overpowered the captain. They turned the ship and sailed in the opposite direction, to Spain. Magellan waited for the missing ship, but then went on without it. He would never see it again.

The expedition sped north, along the coast of South America. After 900 miles, Magellan began to veer west. In a few days, he thought, they would reach the Spice Islands.

"No Relief or Refreshment of Any Kind"

t night, the five stars of the Southern Cross drenched the ships with ghostly light. Dawn brought pale skies, dark water, and feathery clouds.

The days and nights dragged on. For three months and twenty days, the fleet kept sailing. But not once did they ever sight land.

There was, wrote Pigafetta, "no relief or refreshment of any kind."

Each day, their plight grew worse. Their food supply slowly rotted. Biscuits crumbled into handfuls of dust. Barrels of drinking water went

foul. Starving sailors began to peel leather from the ship's rigging. Soaking the leather in salt water made it soft enough to eat. A roasted mouse was worth a fortune.

Before long, scurvy broke out. The disease was worse than hunger and thirst. It made the sailors' gums swell up so that they were unable to eat. In his log, Pigafetta recorded the deaths. Nineteen men died from swollen gums. "Twenty-five or thirty men fell sick in the arms, legs, or in another place," he wrote, "so that few remained well."

One day, in early March, a shout suddenly rang out. "Land ho! Land ho!" called a lookout. "God be praised!" His words electrified the crews. All they could think about was going ashore and finding food and water.

But it was a false alarm. The land turned out to be a few desert islands. There was no point even in stopping. The men could not hide their despair. Magellan ordered the fleet to pass by the "Unfortunate Islands," as he called them.

The Pacific winds filled the sails. The fleet drove westward until it came to another group of islands. These were the Marianas. The largest of them is Guam. To Magellan's relief, the island was inhabited. People could be seen on the beach.

Never had he expected the crossing to take so long. Of course, he now realized that Serrão was mistaken. The Spice Islands did not lie close to the

Americas. Instead, they were located on the opposite side of an enormous ocean.

Everybody felt overjoyed to see land at last. But they approached with caution. Would the natives be friendly? They soon found out. To their horror, the islands were full of thieves. These crooks struck at night. In their canoes, they boldly glided up to the ships. They crept on board and stole everything they could carry away. Once they even took the *Victoria*'s lifeboat.

The theft of the lifeboat was a serious matter. Putting out to sea without a lifeboat was dangerous. And besides, Magellan had lost patience with the greedy savages. A band of his men landed with guns. They regained the stolen goods. Then they burned down the natives' huts. Seven islanders lost their lives.

It seemed clear that the Island of Thieves was not a healthy place to remain. After taking food and water on board, the fleet quickly put to sea again. Some 900 miles later, Magellan reached Samar, in the Philippines.

Once again, there was a crowd of men and women standing on the beach. Were they friendly or not? The bad experience with the thieves of the Marianas made Magellan extra careful. He decided not to land on Samar.

Instead, he chose a nearby island, which was uninhabited. Magellan realized that everyone

needed a rest. On the deserted island, his men would be able to recover their health in peace. Many of them were sick or exhausted after the miserable voyage across the Pacific. The ill were taken off the ships. Two tents were erected especially for them. Each day, Magellan stopped to visit.

On the second day, visitors appeared from the neighboring island of Homonohon. Unlike the savages in the Marianas, these people were very kind. They brought gifts of coconuts, oranges, hens, and plum wine. Restored by fresh food and rest, the sick sailors soon regained their strength. Before long, exploring parties were setting out to visit other islands. This marked the first time that Europeans had ever landed in the Philippine Islands.

One of the islands visited was Mindanao, where the natives also welcomed the arrival of strangers. These people were extremely handsome. Well fed, with olive-colored skin, they dressed themselves in skimpy loincloths. Their bodies were perfumed with sweet-smelling oils. They liked heavy earrings and precious bracelets. At their waists gleamed daggers and gleaming gold swords. Some carried heavy shields.

In spite of the weapons, the people of Mindanao were not warlike. Their main occupation was fishing. They were skilled at catching fish from boats by using harpoons and nets.

At the sight of the gold jewelry and swords, the sailors' eyes began to pop. They began to trade various kinds of trinkets for food, spices, and occasionally nuggets of gold. The natives were easy-going and trusting. Of course, they did not realize they were getting the worst of the bargain.

But Magellan was concerned. He warned his men, "No one should risk offending them." In years to come, he foresaw Spanish ships making regular trips to the Moluccas. These islands, he decided, would make a perfect base. Therefore, it was important to stay on good terms with the natives.

Magellan also decided to make friends with the local king. On Good Friday, 1521, the king arrived to pay a call on Magellan. The king and eight men landed in a large boat. Coming on board the *Trinidad*, he embraced Magellan. Then he presented gifts: three porcelain pots that contained rice and tasty yellow fish.

To show his goodwill, Magellan also offered presents. To the king he gave a red and yellow robe. And the king's men received knives and mirrors. Everyone sat down to share a meal together. Magellan let the king know that he wished to be a "casi casi," which meant brother in the native language.

Afterwards, the king's party was given a tour of the ship. The islanders showed much curiosity

about the ship's guns. So a cannon was fired to show
the tremendous power of the weapons.

Then, Magellan began telling the king about
the voyage. He related how they had discovered the
strait between the two great oceans. As he spoke, his
eyes filled with tears, recorded Pigafetta. Even the
memory of that day filled him with joy. The king was
deeply touched by Magellan's story.

In the Philippines, a change seemed to come
over Magellan. One of his goals had been achieved.
Now, he had time to think of other matters.
Magellan had always been a faithful son of the
Catholic Church. But so far, he had shown no

interest in spreading the religion. In Patagonia or
the Marianas, for example, he had not tried to
convert the natives.

But in the Philippines, he revealed the
spiritual side of his character. Perhaps this was
caused by the people themselves. He was surprised
and pleased by their friendliness. Maybe he could
sense that they were ready to adopt a new faith.

On Easter Sunday, Mass was held. Standing
near Magellan, the king recited the Pater Noster
(Our Father) and the Ave Maria (Hail Mary). He was
then baptized, along with his wife, the members of
his court, and about 800 of his subjects.

As the Spanish traveled about the islands, more tribes came to know them as peaceful and fair. At the island of Cebu, Magellan stopped for fresh water and food before heading for the Moluccas. He decided to impress the islanders. Like a thundering god, he sailed up to their shore with flags flying and cannons firing.

This dramatic entrance scared the king of Cebu at first. However, he managed to collect himself. He sent a message to Magellan. Before the ships could land, the king warned, they would have to pay a tribute. Everyone arriving at Cebu paid. Why should the Spanish be an exception?

Without hesitation, Magellan refused. "The king of Spain pays tribute to no man," he declared. "Tell your king that we come in peace and not in war. But if he wants war, he shall have fire and destruction!"

This threat was delivered to the king of Cebu. He was still shaking at the sight of the smoking cannons. Without further argument, he agreed to forget about the payment of tribute. Just the opposite. The king offered to pay tribute to Magellan. Food and supplies were promised. Conversion to Christianity was also mentioned.

As a sign of peace, gifts were exchanged. Finally, Magellan went ashore to visit the king. He was accompanied by some of his crew, who unloaded their knickknacks and set up a market. Before long, a brisk business was in progress. Pearls and mirrors were being exchanged for rice, pigs, goats, and any object made of gold. Some of the sailors made fortunes for themselves in the course of one afternoon.

Magellan took no part in the trading. His main concern was to win the local king's respect for the king of Spain. His other objective was to convert the island of Cebu to Christianity. In both of these aims, he had enormous success. On Sunday, April 14, the islanders burned their religious statues in front of a large iron cross. Then, they were baptized by the fleet's chaplain.

Less successful were Magellan's efforts on the nearby island of Mactan. Two tribes and two chiefs lived there. One chief was named Zula, the other Silapulapu. This pair had no intention of accepting Christianity or swearing loyalty to the Spanish king. They decided to prepare a trap for Magellan.

First, however, they had to get him off the ship with all those deadly cannons. How could they lure him to Mactan? A plan was devised.

Zula sent a messenger to speak with Magellan. Chief Zula was ready to become a Christian and pay tribute, the messenger declared. But, there was a dilemma. If Zula did so, Chief Silapulapu would become angry and punish him.

The messenger went on to offer a solution to the dilemma. Magellan was invited to visit Mactan.

"Come to our island and help us to conquer Silapulapu," the crafty messenger said. "We would be very grateful to be free of that terrible man." In fact, one boatload of armed sailors would be plenty. Zula's men would be waiting to join in the fight.

Without hesitation, Magellan agreed. The rebellious Mactans lacked the proper respect for Europeans. It was a good chance to teach them a lesson. And there was no doubt about which side would win. With Western guns, success was virtually guaranteed. To be on the safe side, however, Magellan decided to invade Mactan with sixty armed men in three boats.

It was time to leave. The men began to strap on their armor. They wore breastplates and helmets made of steel. Their weapons included swords, spears, daggers, and muskets. Aboard the *Trinidad*, the officers were shocked when they saw Magellan pulling on his armor. "Not you!" someone cried, "You should stay on board."

None of the men believed they would be injured. After all, Silapulapu and his warriors had no guns. Their weapons were practically toys, compared to those of the Europeans. Still, nobody thought it was a good idea for Magellan to fight. His life was too precious to risk, they argued.

But Magellan refused to listen. Stubborn as always, he replied, "Perhaps the shepherd should abandon his flock when there is a wolf nearby?"

Nothing could persuade him to stay behind.

At midnight, the men climbed into the boats. Among the group were several natives—a king who had recently become a Christian and some of his tribesmen. Quickly, the three boats were lowered to the water. The men began to row away.

The native king and his men smiled. They pointed in the direction of Mactan. Soon, they began to chant a mournful song.

On April 27, 1521, at three o'clock in the morning, the boats reached the shore of Mactan. They were unable to land, however. Along the water's edge, the seabed was covered with jagged rocks. There was the risk of tearing holes in the bottoms of the boats.

Besides, Magellan was in no rush. Before attacking, he decided to give Silapulapu another chance. The message was borne by an islander who spoke the language.

In the dim light before the dawn, the warriors of Zula and Silapulapu poured onto the shore. Aroused by their watchmen, they knew the invaders had come. The beach was crowded with men carrying shields and spears.

The mood of the Mactan warriors was ugly. Silapulapu had just delivered a fiery warning. The foreigners, he told his men, would turn them into slaves. If they gave in to Magellan, their freedom would vanish.

By the time that Magellan's messenger arrived, the Mactans were stirred up. Nevertheless, they crowded around to hear the messenger's words. He reminded them of the foreigners' power. It would be foolish to resist. Why not honor the king of Spain and pay the tribute that Magellan demanded? With food and supplies, the fleet would soon be on its way to the Moluccas.

Silapulapu would not budge. "If you have spears that cut well, and armor and guns, we, too, have weapons that bring death to our enemies."

"Is that your reply?"

"Go and tell your master what I have said," Silapulapu ordered. When Magellan heard Silapulapu's challenge, he knew that bloodshed could not be avoided. As dawn was breaking, he leaped into the water. At the head of his men, he began wading toward shore. He hoped that the sight of the armored men with their guns would frighten Silapulapu. Instead, a nasty surprise awaited Magellan.

As he drew closer, he realized that Zula was a traitor. The Mactan chief who had promised to be his ally was with Silapulapu. Behind the two chiefs stood 1,500 excited warriors, itching to fight. Magellan and his men were outnumbered twenty-five to one.

The battle began. Spears and knives flew through the air. Muskets opened fire.

But from the outset, the Mactans seemed to have all the advantages on their side. Their position was stronger. They were on land.

The Spanish were caught wading through the water. Their gunners kept losing their footing and could not shoot straight. By the time the gunners did manage to reach the shore, many were wounded and could not fire their weapons.

The Mactans fought shrewdly. They aimed for the faces of their enemy, which were exposed below the metal helmets. And they knew how to use their spears to ward off the knives and pikes.

Magellan had an idea. He signaled some of his men to set fire to the Mactan village. He hoped they would flee and try to save their burning homes. Unfortunately, his strategy backfired. When Silapulapu noticed the fires, he shouted, "They are destroying your houses. Make them pay for it! Kill! Kill!" His men attacked with even greater ferocity.

Magellan was forced to order a retreat. This time, he was recognized.

Silapulapu pointed. "Their leader! Don't let him escape!" The Mactans lunged forward. Their spears struck Magellan in the face. He stumbled and fell.

When his men rushed to help, he warned them off. "Save your lives," he gasped. "That's an order." His voice was faint. His face had turned deathly pale.

Wading to the boats, the Spaniards fought to defend themselves. Most were able to escape. The dead left behind included nine sailors and four islanders.

Seeing that Magellan had fallen, the Mactans continued to stab him until he was dead.

For the great explorer, the voyage was over. He had led his crew through some of the worst hardships ever faced by an expedition. And then, he had been slain on a small island, at the hands of a proud, warlike people. No crueler trick of fate can be imagined.

The crew aboard Magellan's fleet could not believe that their captain was dead. The officers sent a messenger to Silapulapu. They offered to buy back Magellan's body. But the Mactan chief refused. He understood Magellan's worth.

To this day, nobody knows exactly what happened to Magellan's remains.

The *Victoria* Sails Around the World

The death of Magellan stunned his followers. Plans were made to leave Cebu at once. So rushed was the departure that one man was left stranded on the shore. His pleas to be taken aboard were ignored.

By now, only three ships remained. But there were not enough men left to sail them. It was decided to sink the *Concepcion*, which was the least seaworthy. After all valuables had been removed, it was burned.

The *Trinidad* and the *Victoria* set sail for the Spice Islands. When the ships finally dropped anchor in the harbor at Tidore, there was great rejoicing on board. After almost two years at sea, they had reached their true destination at last.

To their relief, there was no trouble. The local people welcomed the chance to trade. Spices and silks were exchanged for European goods.

Before long, the holds of the ships were filling up with precious goods. But during the loading, disaster struck. Suddenly, the *Trinidad* sprang a leak. The calamity seemed to throw the Spanish officers into panic. It seemed doubtful that the

Trinidad could ever complete the voyage. Eager to be gone, they decided to proceed without her.

But Magellan's flagship was not to be abandoned in the Spice Islands. A new plan was hastily devised. Once the ship was repaired, her crew was supposed to sail back across the Pacific to America. For some reason, the Spanish believed this voyage would be easier than following the *Victoria* around India and Africa. They were wrong.

The route assigned to the *Trinidad* turned out to be impossible. From the very outset, the ship ran into trouble. The winds were blowing in the wrong direction. The captain could make no headway at all. In desperation, he turned back toward the Spice Islands. But more bad luck followed. The entire crew was seized by the Portuguese. They were treated as outlaws and thrown into prison.

The Portuguese argued that the Spanish had no business being in the Spice Islands. They based this belief on the line of demarcation set by the Treaty of Tordesillas. The Portuguese insisted that the Moluccas fell on their side of the line. As it turned out, their calculations were correct. Magellan's voyage proved it by establishing the real width of the Pacific.

The crew of the *Trinidad* suffered an unhappy fate. Some perished in prison. Others were set free and then died. A few chose to remain in the islands. Only four members of the crew returned to Spain.

The *Trinidad* itself vanished from history. Did the Portuguese strip her of timber and instruments before destroying her? Or did she go to the bottom in another attempt to make her seaworthy? The *Trinidad's* fate remains a mystery.

Only the *Victoria* was left. Under Juan Sebastian del Cano, it set out bravely on the long voyage home. Del Cano was unable to take a northern route to Malacca, where the ship might have been captured by the Portuguese. Instead, he turned south of Java toward the open sea.

Del Cano was an experienced navigator. But of all routes he might have chosen, this was the longest and most dangerous. To avoid the enemy, he had to cross the Indian Ocean at its widest point. There was no other choice.

"Death is better than a Portuguese prison," Del Cano warned his men. Nobody argued.

Still, some of them died just the same. They succumbed to hunger or disease. The rest suffered horribly.

Week after week, Del Cano struggled to maneuver the ship. The *Victoria* sailed across the southern tip of Africa, where it rounded the Cape of Good Hope. Slowly, it limped up the west coast of Africa. Most of the crew lacked the strength to sail the ship.

Finally, the *Victoria* reached the Portuguese Cape Verde Islands. Del Cano was forced to risk a

landing. The need for food and water had become desperate. Lying, he told the authorities that he had been sailing in Spanish waters. But the truth came out. The Portuguese found out that the ship was carrying a cargo of spices from the Moluccas.

In a hair-raising escape, Del Cano fled before he lost his ship. The unlucky sailors who had gone ashore were arrested.

On September 6, 1522, the *Victoria* entered the harbor of San Lucar de Barrameda. The sole survivor of Magellan's fleet was home after three years. On September 20, 1519, hundreds of men had left that very same harbor aboard the fleet of five vessels. Eighteen men came back.

Word of the *Victoria's* return spread rapidly. An immense crowd jammed the dock when the ship reached Seville. As the survivors came ashore, cheers rang out. But many people wept as well.

Emperor Charles V summoned Del Cano to the court. "Where is Magellan?" he asked the captain.

"Dead, your Majesty."

The emperor's face saddened. He fell silent. "Well," he murmured, "his name will live in history."

Charles V was right. Magellan had promised to circle the globe. The great circumnavigator did not live to enjoy his triumph. But the *Victoria* came home to prove the truth of his grand vision.

The Death of Ferdinand Magellan

When we reached land, those men had formed in three divisions to the number of more than one thousand five hundred persons. When they saw us, they charged down upon us with exceedingly loud cries, two divisions on our flanks and the other on our front. When the captain saw that, he formed us into two divisions, and thus did we begin to fight.

The musketeers and crossbowmen shot from a distance for about a half hour, but uselessly; for the shots only passed through the shields which were made of thin wood and the arms (of the bearers). The captain cried to them, "Cease firing! Cease firing," but his order was not heeded at all. When the natives saw that we were shooting our muskets to no purpose, crying out they determined to stand firm, for they redoubled their shouts.

When our muskets were discharged, the natives would never stand still, but leaped hither and thither, covering themselves with their shields. They shot so many arrows at us and hurled so many bamboo spears (some of them tipped with iron) at the captain-general, besides pointed stakes hardened with fire, stones, and mud, that we could scarcely defend ourselves.

Seeing that, the captain-general sent some men to burn their houses in order to terrify them. When they saw their houses burning, they were roused to greater fury. Two of our men were killed near the houses, while we burned twenty or thirty houses. So many of them charged down upon us that they shot the captain through the right leg with a poisoned arrow. On that account, he ordered us to retire slowly, but the men took to flight, except six or eight of us who remained with the captain. . . . So we continued to retire for more than a good crossbow flight from the shore, always fighting up to our knees in water.

The natives continued to pursue us, and picking up the same spear four or five times, hurled it again and again. Recognizing the captain, so many turned upon him that they knocked his helmet off his head twice, but he always stood firmly like a good knight, together with some others. Thus did we fight for more than one hour, refusing to retire further.

An Indian hurled a bamboo spear into the captain's face but the latter immediately killed him with his lance, which he left in the Indian's body. Then, trying to lay hand on sword, he could draw it out but halfway, because he had been wounded in the arm with a bamboo spear. When the natives saw that, they all hurled themselves upon him. One of them wounded him on the left leg with a large cutlass, which resembles a scimitar, only being larger. That caused the captain to fall face downward, when immediately they rushed upon him with iron and bamboo spears, and also with their cutlasses, until they killed our mirror, our light, our comfort, and our true guide. When they wounded him, he turned back many times to see whether we were all in the boats.

Thereupon, beholding him dead, we, wounded, retreated, as best as we could to the boats, which were already pulling off.

FROM Antonio Pigafetta's *Voyage*

Antonio Pigafetta— Magellan's Diarist

Antonio Pigafetta was one of the eighteen men who circumnavigated the globe. He began the voyage aboard Magellan's flagship, the *Trinidad*. He finished it aboard the *Victoria,* the only ship of the fleet to complete the voyage envisioned by Magellan. His work, *The First Voyage Around the World,* is the best account of what happened along the way.

Pigafetta came from Vicenza, in Venetian territory, where he was born about the year 1491. Little is known about him before 1519, when he sailed with Magellan. Because of his writing ability, Magellan assigned him to keep a diary of their time at sea. This diary was the basis of the book Pigafetta published after the *Victoria* returned to Spain.

His book is a moving tribute to Magellan, whom he calls "so noble a captain." It is also a valuable record of the islands and their inhabitants which he saw in the East Indies.

The following passage, concerning one experience in the Philippine Islands, is a good example of his method:

Until the supper was brought in, the King with two of his chiefs and two of his beautiful women drank the contents of a large jar of palm wine without eating anything. I, excusing myself as I had supped, would only drink but once....

Then the supper, which consisted of rice and very salty fish, and served in porcelain dishes, was brought in. They ate their rice as if it were bread, which they cook in the following manner. They first put in an earthen jar like our jars, a large leaf which lines all of the jar. Then they add the water

The Marianas, or the Islands of Thieves, as illustrated in the margin of Pigafetta's book. A typical Polynesian boat can be seen.

and rice, and after covering it, allow it to boil until the rice becomes as hard as bread, when it is taken out in pieces. Rice is cooked in the same way throughout those districts.

When we had eaten, the King had a reed mat and another of palm leaves, and a leaf pillow, brought in so that I might sleep on them. The King and his two women went to sleep in a separate place, while I slept with one of the chiefs.

When day came and until the dinner was brought in, I walked about the island. I saw many articles of gold in those houses but little food. After that, we dined on rice and fish, and at the conclusion of dinner, I asked the King by signs whether I could see the Queen.

He replied that he was willing, and we went together to the summit of a lofty hill, where the Queen's house was located. When I entered the house, I made a bow to the Queen, and she did the same to me, whereupon I sat down beside her. She was making a sleeping mat of palm leaves. In the house there were hanging a number of porcelain jars and four metal gongs—one of which was larger than the second, while the other two were still smaller—for playing upon. There were many male and female slaves who served her.

The Lusiads: A Poem About the Great Portuguese Navigators

Fifty years after Magellan's voyage, Luiz Vaz de Camões wrote an epic poem celebrating Portugal as the mother of great navigators. He called his poem *The Lusiads,* meaning "The Sons of Lusus," the mythical founder of Portugal.

Camões (1524-1580), born two years after the *Victoria* returned home, saw much of the growing Portuguese Empire. Like Magellan, he served in North Africa and India. He was in China, Southeast Asia, and East Africa. What he witnessed made him realize the tremendous feat of his fellow countrymen in discovering new lands, building forts and trading stations around the world, and controlling populations larger than that of Portugal itself.

Camões had been aboard sailing ships buffeted by storms at the Cape of Good Hope, and painfully sailed the Indian Ocean under a torrid sun. He had seen Portuguese viceroys governing foreign peoples, and Portuguese explorers pushing beyond the frontiers of the known world. The spectacle moved him to admiration and patriotism. He put both admiration and patriotism into *The Lusiads,* which he published in 1572. The following lines from his epic poem indicate how he felt about his homeland and its adventurers:

A fifteenth-century print of *The Great Voyages*
of Theodore de Bry. The ships from western
countries sailed all the seas of the world in the
Age of Discovery.

Arms, and those matchless chiefs who from the shore
Of Western Lusitania (Portugal) began
To track the oceans none had sailed before,
Yet past Tapróbané's (Sri Lanka's) far limit ran,
And daring every danger, every war,
With courage that excelled the powers of Man,
Amid remotest nations caused to rise
Young empire which they carried to the skies;

So, too, good memory of those kings who went
Afar, religion and our rule to spread;
And who, through either hateful continent,
Africa or Asia, like destruction sped;
And theirs, whose valiant acts magnificent
Saved them from the dominion of the dead,
My song shall sow through the world's every part,
So help me this my genius and my art....

Love of country, thou shalt see, not dominated
By vile reward but a deathless thing and high.
My prize must not be basely estimated,
Who still my native land would magnify.
Hark and behold their glory celebrated,
Whose lord thou art at height of sovranty,
And thou shalt judge which is the better case,
To rule the earth or govern such a race.

FROM *The Lusiads*
WRITTEN BY **Luiz de Camões**
TRANSLATED BY **Leonard Bacon**
(The Hispanic Society of New York, 1950)

The Diary
of a Genoese Pilot

There was a pilot, from Genoa, Italy, aboard Magellan's flagship, the *Trinidad,* who, like Pigafetta, kept a diary during the voyage. We are not sure of this pilot's name. The best guess is that he was Leone Pancaldo. His *Diary* is priceless, because without it we would know little or nothing about the fate of the *Trinidad*, which was damaged in the Moluccas and could not sail with the *Victoria*. The men aboard the *Trinidad* tried, after repairing their ship, to return to Europe from the west. They hoped to retrace the outward voyage of Magellan's fleet, and to reach America by way of the Pacific.

It was a rash decision, leading to disaster. After a terrible voyage into the Pacific, the *Trinidad* had to return to the Moluccas with a crew decimated by starvation, thirst, and illness.

At the Moluccas, the Portuguese, under Antonio de Brito, imprisoned all the sailors. A few managed to escape and return to their homelands after many years. Among those, fortunately for us, was the Genoese pilot. Here is his passage on the end of the *Trinidad:*

They ran out of bread, wine, meat, and oil, and found themselves with only rice and water. The cold was intense and they had no proper clothing. The men began to die. When this happened, they decided to return to the Moluccas, and did so as quickly as they could. When they were still five hundred leagues away, they tried to land on the island of Magregua, but were unable to do so because it was night. They waited until the following

An old engraving of the *Victoria*, one of the five ships of Magellan's fleet—the only one to complete the mission and return home safely

morning, but still did not succeed. They then
tried Dhomi and Batechina. When they had
dropped their anchor, a boat came up
containing several men, among whom was
the chief of an island called Geilolo. He
informed them that the Portuguese were
building a fortress in the Moluccas.

When they learned this, they sent a boat
with some men to the Portuguese commander,
Antonio de Brito, to ask him to come and get
their ship. They said that most of the crew
were dead, the rest ill, and the ship could not
be manned. When De Brito saw the message
and looked at the map, he sent Garcia
Amriquiz, captain of the San Giorgio, *to look*
for the ship. When they found it, they brought
it back to the fortress. While it was being
unloaded, a storm blew in from the north and
drove it onto the shore.

HISTORICAL CHRONOLOGY

Life of Magellan	Historical and Cultural Events
1480 Born of a noble, country family in Portugal.	

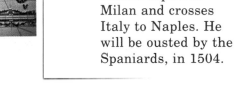

The entry of Louis XII into Naples—a fifteenth-century miniature

	1488 The Portuguese navigator Bartholomew Dias rounds the Cape of Good Hope to East Africa.
	1492 Christopher Columbus lands in America on the island of Guanahani.
	1494 A new demarcation line between Spanish and Portuguese territory is established by the Treaty of Tordesillas.
	1497 John Cabot and his son, Sebastian, explores the coast of North America.
	1499 King Louis XII of France captures Milan and crosses Italy to Naples. He will be ousted by the Spaniards, in 1504.

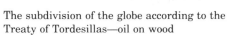

The subdivision of the globe according to the Treaty of Tordesillas—oil on wood

Life of Magellan	Historical and Cultural Events
1505 Sails with an expedition under Francisco de Alameida; he is wounded in the Battle of Diu.	**1505** Leonardo da Vinci works on his famous portrait, *Mona Lisa,* also known as the *Gioconda.*
	1508 Michelangelo begins the frescoes in the Sistine Chapel, at the request of Pope Julius II.
1511 In the service of Alfonso de Albuquerque, he is present at the conquest of Malacca; he is made an officer for his bravery.	

The departure of Magellan's fleet—a sixteenth-century engraving

Leonardo da Vinci, *Mona Lisa*, also known as *Gioconda*

Life of Magellan	Historical and Cultural Events
1513 Repatriated to Lisbon because of hostility of his superiors; they resent his criticism.	**1513** Niccolo Machiavelli writes *The Prince*, his masterpiece on political philosophy.

1514 Sent as a soldier to Africa to fight against the Moors, and is wounded in the Battle of Asimur; he will limp for the rest of his life; returns to Lisbon to defend himself against the charge of having sold "war booty" to the enemy; rehabilitated, he retires from public life and devotes himself to nautical and cosmo-graphical study.

Francis I, king of France, on horseback—painted at the end of the sixteenth century

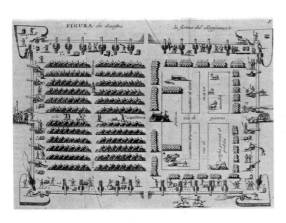

Niccolo Machiavelli, a chart from *The Art of War*

A view of James Bay, in the southern area of Hudson Bay

Life of Magellan	Historical and Cultural Events
1515 Encouraged by letters from his friend Francisco Serrão in the Moluccas, he conceives the idea of searching for a southwest passage from the Atlantic to the Pacfic.	**1515** Francis I becomes king of France and wins the Battle of Marignano, giving him control of Milan; he will challenge Charles V, the Holy Roman Emperor, for supremacy in Italy; loses the Battle of Pavia (1525), leaving Charles triumphant.
	1516 Sebastian Cabot accepts a commission from the king of Spain to explore in the direction of Hudson Bay.
1517 Discusses passage idea with astronomer Ruy Faleiro, but King Manuel I of Portugal refuses financial assistance, and he goes to Spain.	**1517** Martin Luther nails his 95 theses on a church door in Wittenberg, the start of his break with the Catholic Church.
1518 Under the protection of the young King Charles I of Spain, and with financing from private interests, he is able to get his project underway.	

Life of Magellan	Historical and Cultural Events
1519 Sets out from San Lucar de Barrameda on September 20 with a fleet of five ships; *Trinidad* (his flagship), *San Antonio, Concepcion, Victoria,* and *Santiago.*	**1519** Hernando Cortez, the cruel Spanish conqueror, lands in Mexico and in two years has wrested power from Montezuma in the Aztec Empire; Montezuma is killed by his own people, as he attempts to head off a revolution.

Hernando Cortez at the Battle of Otumba, in Mexico—anonymous painting

Raphael, *The Madonna of the Cardellino*

The Strait of Magellan and the Land of the Giants—a map by Sebastian Munster

Life of Magellan	Historical and Cultural Events
1520 Having crossed the Atlantic and stopped briefly at Brazil, he reaches the River Plate on January 10; arrives on March 31 at Port San Julian, where he spends the winter; the *Santiago* is lost while exploring the coast; he suppresses a mutiny among his captains; the *San Antonio* abandons the fleet and returns to Spain; he discovers the strait leading from the Atlantic into the Pacific on October 21; it is now called the "Strait of Magellan"; he and his men notice the star formations, now called the "Clouds of Magellan."	**1520** Raphael dies, only 37 years old; his most important paintings include portraits of Julius II and Leo X, the Sistine Chapel's *Madonna*, and the *Madonna of the Cardellino*. Charles V is crowned Holy Roman Emperor.

Raphael, *Pope Leo X with Cardinals*

Titian, *Portrait of the Emperor Charles V*

Life of Magellan	Historical and Cultural Events
1521 After a harrowing voyage across the Pacific, he reaches the Marianas and the Philippines. He lands on a number of islands in the name of the king of Spain, imposes a tribute, and has some local people baptized. Leaders on the island of Mactan reject his demands; he leads a landing party, and is killed in a skirmish on April 27.	**1521** Martin Luther is condemned by the Diet of Worms, after being excommunicated by Pope Leo X. He seeks refuge with Frederick of Saxony, and begins a German translation of *The Bible*. Emperor Charles V condemns Luther, and forbids the distribution of his writings. The Ottoman Empire, under Suleiman I—"The Magnificent"—reaches the height of its power, extending beyond the Danube to Belgrade. King Manuel I—"The Fortunate"—of Portugal dies; during his reign, voyages of exploration reached Brazil and the East Indies.

Amber in Jaipur, India, the Temple of Jagat Shromani or Vishnu—Mogul architecture

Life of Magellan	Historical and Cultural Events
1522 The *Victoria* returns to San Lucar on September 6; under Sebastian del Cano, she has crossed the Indian Ocean and rounded the Cape of Good Hope—a practical demonstration that the earth is a sphere; European cartographers draw up new maps of the world, using information from this voyage; the size of the Pacific Ocean is recognized for the first time.	**1522** Ulrich Zwingli publishes two tracts attacking the Catholic Church; they give momentum to the Reformation in Switzerland.
1523 Pigafetta, using his notes from aboardship, writes *The First Voyage Around the World*, giving a graphic account of Magellan and his achievement.	

The beach at Mactan—where Magellan was killed

Life of Magellan	Historical and Cultural Events

Henry VIII of England—portrait by Holbein | **1526** Saint Ignatius Loyola writes his *Spiritual Exercises*, which becomes the basic religious book of the Jesuit Order.

Babur founds the Mogul Empire, in India. |
| | **1527** Henry VIII asks the Pope for an annulment of his marriage to Catherine of Aragon, in order to legalize his relationship with Anne Boleyn; when the Pope refuses, he severs all relations with the Catholic Church. |

A view of the Cape of Good Hope—rounded by the *Victoria* on its voyage home

BOOKS FOR FURTHER READING

The Explorers by Richard Humble, Time-Life Books, 1978.

The First Men Around the World by Andrew Langley, Silver Burdett, 1982.

The First Ships Round the World by Walter Brownlee, Cambridge University Press, 1974.

Ferdinand Magellan by Alan Blackwood, Franklin Watts, 1986.

Ferdinand Magellan by Ruth Harley, Troll, 1979.

Ferdinand Magellan: *Noble Captain* by Katherine Wilkie, Houghton-Mifflin, 1963.

Ferdinand Magellan: *A World Explorer* by Lynn Groh, Garrard, 1963.

Magellan's Voyage Around the World: Three Contemporary Accounts edited by Charles E. Nowell, Northwestern University Press, 1962.

INDEX

(Continued on page 104)